W9-CEN-969

JOURNEYS

Close Reader

GRADE 1

Consumable

UNIT 1
Around the Neighborhood

UNIT 2
Sharing Time

UNIT 3
Nature Near and Far

UNIT 4
Exploring Together

UNIT 5
Watch Us Grow

UNIT 6
Three Cheers for Us!

JOURNEYS

Close Reader

UNIT 1
Around the Neighborhood

Background Friends use different words when they greet each other. They also use different words to show that they like and care for each other.

Setting a Purpose Read to find out what <u>jambo</u> means.

Jambo

by Sundaira Morninghouse

① Read Circle the words that tell what <u>jambo</u> means.

Jambo

Jambo Jambo
ambo ambo
mbo mbo
bo bo bo
o o o
bo bo bo
mbo mbo
ambo ambo
Jambo Jambo
HI! HELLO!
Did you Did you
did you know
Jambo means
hello hello!

SHORT RESPONSE

Cite Text Evidence Reread the poem. What do you notice about the words <u>Jambo</u>, <u>know</u>, and <u>hello</u>?

_____

- -

_____

Background There are different kinds of storms. Scientists study these storms to learn more about them.

Setting a Purpose Read to find out about storms.

Storms!

Read Together

This is a lightning storm.

①Read Underline the sentence that tells what a storm is.

A storm is a strong wind with rain or snow. It may have **hail** or sleet. Warm, light air goes up quickly. It mixes with high, cold air. Look! It's a storm.

hail:

②Reread Reread page 5. Then look at the photograph on page 4. Write what kind of storm is shown in the photograph. Tell how you know.

_____

- -

_____

_____

- -

_____

③ **Read** Underline the text that tells what this page is mostly about.

Kinds of Storms

A thunderstorm has thunder and lightning. It can bring **heavy** rain.

heavy:

A tornado is a strong, twisting wind. It is shaped like a cone.

A hurricane is a very big storm. It has strong, spinning winds and rain.

A dust storm is a strong wind that carries dust for miles.

④ **Reread** Reread page 6. Find the names of different storms. Write them below.

_____

- - - - - - - - - - - - - - - - - -

_____

- - - - - - - - - - - - - - - - - -

_____

⑤ Read Circle the photograph of a thermometer.

Measuring Storms

Scientists use tools to measure. They measure heat and cold. They measure the wind. They measure rainfall and snowfall, too.

What storms have you seen?

thermometer

wind gauge

rain gauge

SHORT RESPONSE

Cite Text Evidence Reread pages 4–7. What did you learn about storms? Write it below.

_____

- - - - - - - - - - - - - - - - - - -

_____

Background Schools long ago were different than they are today. Children didn't have school buses, backpacks, or notebooks.

Setting a Purpose Read to find out how schools were different long ago.

School Long Ago

1 **Read** Underline the word that tells how some children got to school long ago.

How did children get to school?

Was going to school long ago different from going to school today? Let's find out! There were no school buses long ago. Some children had to walk far to get to school.

2 **Reread** Reread page 9. Find out what people didn't have long ago. Write it below.

_____

- -

_____

_____

- -

_____

③ Read How did children carry their books long ago? Circle the photograph.

slates:

What did children take to school?

Long ago, children did not have backpacks. They carried their things for school in their arms. Children did not have a lot of paper long ago. They used chalk to write on small boards called **slates**.

THEN | NOW

④ Reread Reread page 10. Underline the sentence that tells why children used slates to write on.

CLOSE READ
Notes

⑤ Read Underline the words that tell what children learned long ago.

What did children learn?

Long ago, children learned reading, writing, and math. Some teachers taught children funny songs to sing. What do children learn in school today?

SHORT RESPONSE

Cite Text Evidence Reread pages 9–11. What is one way school was different long ago? Write it below.

_____

_____

_____

_____

_____

Background The city and country are different from each other. Some people like the city. Some people like the country.

Setting a Purpose Read to find out what the Country Mouse finds out about the city.

City Mouse and Country Mouse

retold by Debbie O'Brien

Cast

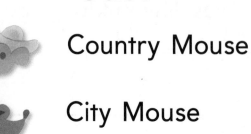

Country Mouse

City Mouse

Cat

CLOSE READ
Notes

①Read Underline the sentence that tells who the story is about.

 Once upon a time, there were two mice.

 I love my country home. Come eat with me.

 I like city food better.

②Reread Reread page 13. Find out what the City Mouse likes. Write it below.

_____

- - - - - - - - - - - - - - - - - -

_____

- - - - - - - - - - - - - - - - - -

_____

③ Read Look for details in the text that tell where the mice go. Circle the name of the place.

 Come with me to the city. We will eat like kings.

 I will come.

 Here is my home.

Look at all this yummy food!

④ Reread Reread page 14. Find what the Country Mouse sees in the city. Write it below.

_____

- -

_____

- -

_____

⑤ Read Look for details in the text that tell who the mice see. Circle the name.

 Meow, **meow**. I will have mice for lunch!

meow:

 Who is that?

 It's Cat! Run and hide.

 City Mouse, my home does not have fine food, but it is safe. I'm going back to the country.

SHORT RESPONSE

Cite Text Evidence Reread pages 12–15. What does the Country Mouse learn about the city? Write it below.

_____

- -

_____

- -

_____

Background Zoos have many different kinds of animals in them. People go there to see animals from different places.

Setting a Purpose Read to find out what kinds of animals are in this city zoo.

City Zoo

Read Together

1 **Read** Circle the name of the place the text tells about.

Welcome to the City Zoo!
The zoo is full of many
interesting animals. See if
you can find all the animals
on the **map** on the next
page.

map:

2 **Reread** Reread page 17. What can you find in the zoo? Write it below.

_____

- -

_____

_____

- -

_____

- -

_____

- -

_____

3 **Read** Circle the picture of the <u>elephant</u> on the map.

Key

tiger

elephant

polar bear

giraffe

4 **Reread** Reread the key on page 18. Which animals does it help you find in the zoo? Underline their names.

18

⑤ Read Circle what you need to hold on to at the zoo.

We hope you have a good time at the zoo.

- Come with your family and a friend.
- Hold on to your ticket.
- Have some snacks.
- Pull a wagon.
- Take pictures.

SHORT RESPONSE

Cite Text Evidence Reread pages 17–19. What is this selection about? Write it below.

_____

- -

_____

_____

- -

_____

_____

- -

_____

19

UNIT 2
Sharing Time

Background People make houses out of different kinds of materials, such as bricks, wood, and even mud. Some of these materials are stronger than others.

Setting a Purpose Read to find out what kinds of houses the three little pigs make.

The Three Little Pigs

① **Read** Underline the words that tell when the story happens.

Once upon a time, there were three little pigs.

The first pig made a **straw** house. Soon he could hear Wolf call out.

"Let me come in," said Wolf.

"No," said the pig.

"I'll huff and I'll puff. I'll blow your house in," Wolf said.

straw:

② **Reread** Reread page 23. What does the first pig use to make his house? Write it below.

_____

- -

_____

③ Read Circle the word that tells what the second pig uses to make his house.

stick:

The second pig made a **stick** house.

"Let me come in," said Wolf.

"No," said the pig.

"I'll huff and I'll puff. I'll blow your house in," Wolf said.

④ Reread Reread page 24. What does the wolf do to the stick house? Write it below.

_____

- - - - - - - - - - - - - - - - - - - -

_____

_____

- - - - - - - - - - - - - - - - - - - -

_____

⑤ **Read** Underline the sentence that tells what happens to the pigs after Wolf runs away.

The third pig got bricks. He used every brick to make a strong house. Wolf could not blow this house in.

Wolf gave up and ran away. The three pigs lived happily ever after.

SHORT RESPONSE

Cite Text Evidence   Reread pages 23–25. Why can't the wolf blow in the brick house? Write it below.

_____

- -

_____

_____

- -

_____

Background There are many kinds of insects all around us. Insects don't talk or write, but they do send messages to each other!

Setting a Purpose Read to find out what kinds of messages insects send and how they send them.

Insect Messages

① **Read** Underline the number of legs an insect has.

An insect is an animal that has six legs. An insect's **body** has three parts. Most insects have wings so they can fly.

body:

② **Reread** Reread page 27. Why do most insects have wings? Write it below.

_____

- -

_____

- -

_____

③ **R**ead Circle the photograph of a <u>mosquito</u>.

honeybee

Why do insects send messages? Some insects, such as mosquitoes, find each other by flying toward the sound that other mosquitoes' wings make. Honeybees can tell other honeybees where there is food. Every kind of insect has ways of sending messages.

mosquito

④ **R**eread Reread page 28. What do honeybees tell other honeybees? Write it below.

_____

- -

_____

_____

- -

_____

⑤ Read Circle the word that names the insects in the photograph.

How do insects send each other messages? Ants touch other ants. Crickets make sounds with their front legs. Fireflies flash light.

The next time you see an insect, watch and listen. It may be sending a message!

ants

SHORT RESPONSE

Cite Text Evidence Reread pages 27–29. What did you learn about insects? Write it below.

_____

- -

_____

- -

_____

- -

_____

- -

_____

Background Many people make music by playing drums. Drums can be different sizes and shapes, but they are all alike in some ways.

Setting a Purpose Read to find out about the parts of a drum and how to make one.

Drums

by Tim Pano

© Houghton Mifflin Harcourt Publishing Company • Image Credit: © Las Cruces Sun-News/Norm Dettlaff/AP Images

① **Read** Underline the words that tell where people play drums.

People around the world play drums. Yolanda Martinez plays drums. She makes drums, too. She sells her drums.

② **Reread** Reread page 31. What three things does Yolanda Martinez do with drums? Write them below.

_____

- - - - - - - - - - - - - - - - - - - -

_____

- - - - - - - - - - - - - - - - - - - -

_____

- - - - - - - - - - - - - - - - - - - -

_____

③ Read Circle the picture of the beater stick.

drumhead:

All drums have a frame. They have a **drumhead**, too. Drummers use a beater stick to play this drum.

Parts of a Drum

frame

drumhead

beater stick

④ Reread Reread page 32. What two parts do all drums have? Write them below.

_____

_____

_____

⑤ Read Underline the detail that tells you what to put on top of an empty can when you make a drum.

Make a Drum

Would you like to make a drum today? Try this.

1. Get an empty coffee can or an oatmeal carton.

2. Tape paper around the sides.

3. Now tape brown paper over the top.

SHORT RESPONSE

Cite Text Evidence   Reread pages 31–33. What did you learn about drums? Write it below.

_____

_____

_____

_____

_____

Background Poems can be silly because of the way the words sound. Some poems have rhyming words. Words that rhyme have the same sounds at the end.

Setting a Purpose Read the poem to find some fun rhyming words.

If You're Silly and You Know It

Read Together

1 **Read** Underline the rhyming words in the poem.

If You're Silly and You Know It

If you're silly and you know it,
say a rhyme — fox, box!

If you're silly and you know it,
say a rhyme — red, sled!

If you're silly and you know it,
then your face will surely show it.

If you're silly and you know it,
say a rhyme — play, hooray!

SHORT RESPONSE

Cite Text Evidence   Reread the poem. When you are silly, what part of you will show it? Write it below.

_____

- -

_____

- -

_____

Background We can show that we are happy in different ways. We might sing, or laugh, or jump up and down.

Setting a Purpose Read the poem to find out what this person does in the morning.

Singing-Time

by Rose Fyleman

1 Read Underline the word that rhymes with head.

Singing-Time

I wake in the morning early

And always, the very first thing,

I poke out my head and I sit up in bed

And I sing and I sing and I sing.

SHORT RESPONSE

Cite Text Evidence   Reread the poem. What does the writer do after sitting up in bed? Write it below.

_____

_____

_____

_____

Nature Near and Far

Background Water is all around us! Sometimes it flows, like the water in a garden hose. Other times it is hard, like an ice cube in a glass.

Setting a Purpose Read to find out about the different forms of water.

Water

Read Together

① **Read** Underline the sentence that tells what all living things have in common.

What is one thing that all living things, whether they are big or little, have in common? They need water to live.

Water comes in different forms. The water you drink is a **liquid**. A liquid flows and takes the shape of the container it is in.

liquid:

② **Reread** Reread page 41. What form is the water that you drink? Write it below.

_____

- -

_____

_____

- -

_____

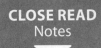

③ **Read** Circle the picture of <u>water</u>.

Water can freeze into ice or snow. Frozen water is a **solid**. A solid has its own shape.

What is ice? Ice is water that has frozen. It is hard and cold.

Where does snow come from? Snow is tiny pieces of frozen water that fall from the clouds.

solid:

water

ice

snow

④ **Reread** Reread page 42. Underline two kinds of solid water.

⑤ Read Underline the name of a place where you could see ice and snow.

Ice and snow are found in many places around the world. The North Pole is one of these places. There is cold, blue water all around it. People cannot live that far north for very long, but some animals make their homes near the North Pole.

SHORT RESPONSE

Cite Text Evidence Reread pages 41–43. What happens to water when it gets very cold? Write it below.

_____

- -

_____

- -

_____

- -

_____

Background Rain forests are very important to our world. They store water and help clean our air. Many different kinds of plants and animals live there, too!

Setting a Purpose Read to find out what you might see in the different parts of a rain forest.

The Rain Forest

Read Together

① **Read** Underline the sentence that tells what the weather is like in a rain forest.

A rain forest is a very wet and warm place. Rain forests have layers. Each layer has its own animals that live in it.

Canopy Layer The tops of trees poking out above the forest form this layer. The tree leaves and branches keep most sunlight off the layers below. Eagles, **sloths**, and monkeys live here.

sloths:

② **Reread** Reread page 45. What animals live in the canopy layer? Write them below.

_____

_____

_____

③ Read What animals live in the understory layer? Circle their names.

Understory Layer This layer is above the ground. It is shady. Young trees and bushes grow here. Frogs, birds, and snakes live here.

tapirs:

Forest Floor Not much sunlight reaches this layer. **Tapirs,** jaguars, and beetles live on the brown forest floor. Ants and giant anteaters also live there. Anteaters have been known to eat thirty thousand insects in a single day!

④ Reread Reread page 46. Which layer of the rain forest is darkest? Write it below.

_____

- -

_____

⑤ Read Circle the name of the place the map key helps you to find on the map.

Do you know where the world's rain forests are? This map shows you.

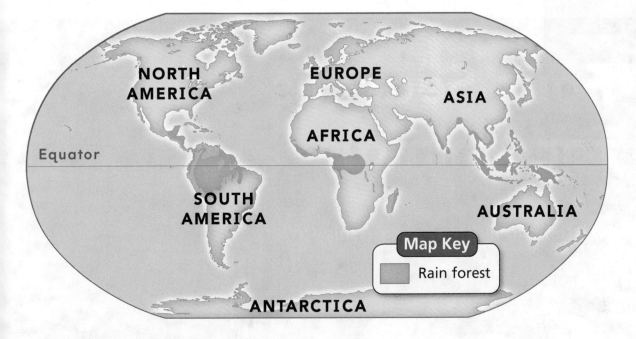

NORTH AMERICA

EUROPE

ASIA

AFRICA

Equator

SOUTH AMERICA

AUSTRALIA

Map Key
Rain forest

ANTARCTICA

SHORT RESPONSE

Cite Text Evidence   Reread pages 45–47. What is one way the layers in a rain forest are different? Write it below.

_____

_____

_____

_____

Background The four seasons are spring, summer, fall, and winter. Every year we have the same seasons in the same order. Animals do different things in each season.

Setting a Purpose Read to find out what happens in each season of the year.

Four Seasons for Animals

Read Together

written and illustrated by Ashley Wolff

① Read Circle the heading for this part of the text.

Spring

It is spring. Young animals run and play. Bird nests are full of eggs. Soon the eggs will hatch.

Spring brings rain. Grass turns green and grows tall. Buds grow on trees and plants. Spring also brings rain puddles! Flower buds get wet. Rain helps the new plants grow.

② Reread Reread page 49. What do young animals do in the spring? Write it below.

_____

- - - - - - - - - - - - - - - - -

_____

- - - - - - - - - - - - - - - - -

_____

③ **Read** Underline the detail that tells what insects do in the summer.

Summer

It is summer. Buds open and flowers bloom in the bright sun. Insects buzz here and there. Now there are chicks in the bird nest! Their mother will teach them how to fly.

It can get very hot in the summer. Many animals live near the pond. Ducks swim in the pond. Fox pups cool off in the shade.

④ **Reread** Reread page 50. What animals swim in the pond? Write it below.

_____

- -

_____

5 **Read** Underline the sentence that tells why some animals eat a lot in the fall.

Fall

It is fall. Leaves fall down. Animals get ready for winter. Some animals eat as much as they can. They need to **store** fat because food is scarce in the winter.

store:

Squirrels and chipmunks gather nuts so they will have enough food for the winter.

6 **Reread** Reread page 51. Which animals collect nuts in the fall? Write them below.

_____

_____

_____

_____

⑦ Read Circle the word that tells where some animals sleep in winter.

Winter

It is winter. Winter can be very cold and wet. Bears hibernate in the winter. That means they sleep.

Many other animals hibernate in the winter. They curl up in dens to keep safe from the cold and wet.

⑧ Reread Reread page 52. What is the heading for this part of the text? Write it below.

_____

- - - - - - - - - - - - - - - - -

_____

⑨ Read Underline the name of the season that will come again after winter.

Like all the seasons, the winter will pass. The animals know that spring will come once again.

SHORT RESPONSE

Cite Text Evidence Reread pages 49–53. Tell about something special that happens in one season. Write it below.

_____

_____

_____

_____

Background There are different kinds of rules and laws. Some help us when we are at home. Others help us when we are away from home.

Setting a Purpose Read to find out how rules and laws help people.

Rules and Laws

Read Together

by J. C. Cunningham

Safety Rule

Health Rule

①Read Underline the heading that tells what this page is mostly about.

Rules

Who needs rules? We all do! Some rules keep us safe and healthy. Some rules help us learn. There are even rules to help us have fun!

Can you find the child following this rule?

Brush your teeth at night.

What other rules are the children following? What could happen if they did not follow the rules?

Game Rule

②Reread Reread pages 54–55. Circle the pictures of a health rule and a game rule.

③ Read Underline the sentence that tells what rules made by the government are called.

Laws

Our government has rules, too. The rules are called laws. Laws keep us safe and healthy. Laws make sure we treat each other fairly.

Traffic Law

④ Reread Reread page 56. What kind of law is shown in the picture? Write it below.

_____

- - - - - - - - - - - - - - - - - - -

_____

5 **Read** Circle the sentence that is a health law.

Can you find the person who obeyed this law?

employees:

Employees must wash hands.

What other laws do you think the pictures show?

Health Law

6 **Reread** Reread page 57. Which person in the picture followed the health law? Write it below.

_____

- -

_____

- -

_____

7 **Read** Underline two details that tell what laws help us become.

citizens:

Laws help us to be good neighbors and good **citizens**.

What laws do you think these people are following? How do the laws help?

8 **Reread** Reread page 58. Look at the picture. Circle the citizens who are obeying a law.

⑨ Read Underline the sentence that tells who needs rules and laws.

Who needs rules and laws? We all do!

SHORT RESPONSE

Cite Text Evidence   Reread pages 55–59. What is one way that rules and laws help people? Write it below.

_____

- -

_____

_____

- -

_____

Background A picnic is a meal that people eat outside. They often pack food from home in a basket and then eat it as they sit on a blanket.

Setting a Purpose Read to find out who comes to a picnic and what food they bring.

Readers' Theater

Animal Picnic

by Debbie O'Brien

Cast of Characters

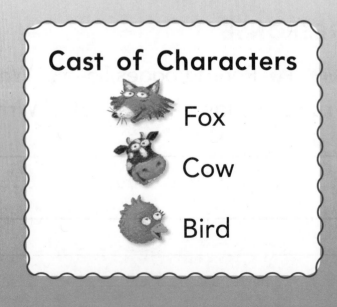

Fox

Cow

Bird

1 **Read** Underline the word that tells how Cow gets to the picnic.

 Hi, Cow and Bird.

How was your trip?

 I had to walk

to get here.

 I had to fly.

2 **Reread** Reread pages 60–61.
Who is the first animal to speak in the play?
Write the animal's name below.

_____

- -

_____

- -

_____

③ Read Circle the words in the play that tell what Fox should do as he talks to Cow.

 (pointing to Cow's basket) What food did you bring for our picnic?

 I brought grass. I use my flat teeth to grind it.

 I brought meat. I use my long, sharp teeth to eat it.

 We both have teeth, but we eat different things!

④ Reread Reread page 62. What food does Cow bring to the picnic? Write it below.

_____

- - - - - - - - - - - - - - - - - - - -

_____

⑤ **Read** Underline the food that Bird brings to the picnic.

 (pointing to Bird's basket)
What did you bring, Bird?

 I did not bring grass or meat. I brought seeds. Birds don't have any teeth!

How will you eat those seeds without teeth?

Watch this!

(Bird eats some seeds.)
Yum, yum, yum!

SHORT RESPONSE

Cite Text Evidence   Reread pages 61–63. Why does Bird say <u>Yum</u>? Write it below.

_____

- -

_____

UNIT 4
Exploring Together

Background It takes hard work to become an astronaut. Astronauts need to learn many things if they want to travel in space.

Setting a Purpose Read to find out important things Mae Jemison did in her life.

Read Together

Mae Jemison

by Debbie O'Brien

① **Read** Underline the sentence that tells what Mae wanted to be when she grew up.

Mae Jemison was born in Alabama. Mae knew she wanted to be a **scientist** when she grew up. Mae studied very hard in college and became a doctor. She went to Africa because she wanted to help sick people there.

scientist:

② **Reread** Reread page 67. Find the place where Mae went after she became a doctor. Write it below.

_____

_ _

_____

67

③ **Read** Look for details in the text that tell what Mae flew to space in. Circle its name.

Later, Mae became an astronaut. She had to learn many things before she could go into space. At last, Mae was ready to fly in the space **shuttle**. The astronauts had to take equipment with them. They had to carry food, too. Mae could move around easily in space. She felt light as a feather.

shuttle:

④ **Reread** Reread page 68. Find things astronauts had to take on the space shuttle. Write them below.

_____

- - - - - - - - - - - - - - - - - - -

_____

- - - - - - - - - - - - - - - - - - -

_____

5 Read Underline the sentence that tells what Mae wants people to do.

Now Mae has her own company. She wants people to think about science. She tries to show people how science helps them every day.

SHORT RESPONSE

Cite Text Evidence Reread pages 67–69. What did you learn about being an astronaut? Write it below.

_____

- -

_____

- -

_____

- -

_____

Background Long ago, there were no paved roads in the western part of North America. Few people knew what the land there was like.

Setting a Purpose Read to learn about the long trip two men took to explore part of North America.

Lewis and Clark's Big Trip

Read Together

Lewis

Clark

① **Read** Underline the sentence that tells the different ways Lewis and Clark traveled.

Meriwether Lewis and William Clark were explorers who traveled across North America many years ago. They walked, rode horses, and traveled by boat. They wrote about their trip in journals.

Lewis and Clark asked an American Indian named Sacagawea to go with them. The **explorers** were sure she could help them talk with other American Indians on the way.

explorers:

② **Reread** Reread page 71. Who helped Lewis and Clark on their trip? Write her name below.

_____

- - - - - - - - - - - - - - - - - - - -

_____

③ Read Underline the words that tell how the people in the village helped Lewis and Clark.

One day they came to an American Indian village. Maybe Sacagawea could speak with the people there. She did, and they gave the explorers supplies and horses.

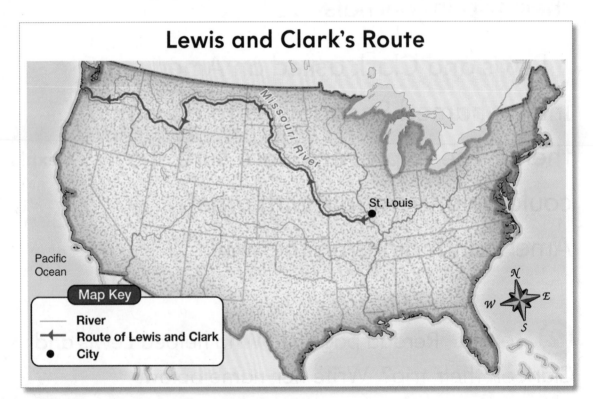

Lewis and Clark's Route

St. Louis

Missouri River

Pacific Ocean

Map Key
— River
←— Route of Lewis and Clark
● City

N E W S

④ Reread Look at the map again. Circle the route Lewis and Clark took.

⑤ Read Underline the words that tell how long it took the explorers to complete their trip.

Sacagawea knew good paths across mountains and through forests. It took the explorers about two years to finish their trip. People can travel the same route today by car.

Sacagawea helps Lewis and Clark.

SHORT RESPONSE

Cite Text Evidence   Reread pages 71–73. What did you learn about Lewis and Clark's route? Write it below.

_____

- - - - - - - - - - - - - - - - - - - -

_____

- - - - - - - - - - - - - - - - - - - -

_____

Background Plants grow from seeds. Beans
are one kind of seed. When a bean is planted
in the ground, a bean plant will grow.

Setting a Purpose Read to find out about
a strange plant that grows from some beans
Jack's mother throws away.

Jack and
the Beanstalk

Read
Together

①Read Underline the words that tell when the story happens.

Once upon a time, there was a boy named Jack. He and his mom had no money for food because someone had taken their goose. Sometimes, it would lay **golden** eggs for them!

golden:

Jack went to sell their cow. He met a man. "I will trade these special beans for your cow," the man said.

②Reread Reread page 75. What does the man trade Jack for his cow? Write it below.

_____

- -

_____

③ Read Underline the sentence that tells where Jack finds his goose.

Jack came home. His mother was mad. She threw the beans on the ground.

Soon a tall beanstalk grew. Jack climbed it. At the top was a huge castle. Inside, Jack found his goose in a cage under a table!

Then Jack heard, "FEE! FIE! FOE! FUM! Look out! Here I come!"

It was a giant! First Jack grabbed the goose. Then he ran right out the door.

④ Reread Reread page 76. Who does Jack run away from? Write it below.

_____

_ _

_____

⑤ Read Underline the sentence that tells what Jack does to the beanstalk.

Jack climbed down the beanstalk as fast as he could. He chopped it down.

Now Jack and his mother were safe, and they had their goose. They all lived happily ever after.

SHORT RESPONSE

Cite Text Evidence   Reread pages 75–77. Why do Jack and his mom live happily ever after? Write it below.

_____

- -

_____

- -

_____

- -

_____

Background Our world is always changing! The things your parents and grandparents saw and used are different from the things you see and use today.

Setting a Purpose Read to find out ways that life has changed for families over the years.

Life Then and Now

① **Read** Underline the detail that tells what helps people to do work today.

The way people live changes over time. Today families live differently than in the past.

In the past, many jobs were done by hand. Now people have machines to help them do work.

In the past, people wrote letters on paper and sent them by mail. Now people can send messages right away. They talk on **cell phones** or send e-mails by computer.

cell phones:

② **Reread** Reread page 79. What are two things people use now to send messages quickly? Write them below.

_____

- -

_____

③ Read Circle the photograph of a <u>car</u> from the past.

In the past, families listened to radio programs. Now families watch TV programs and movies.

Family Life

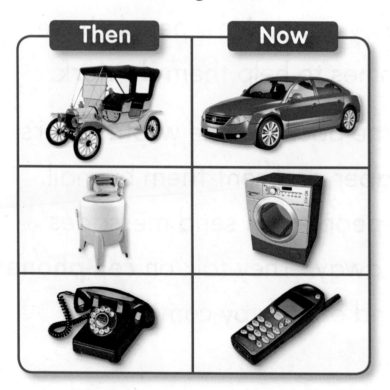

| Then | Now |

④ Reread Reread page 80. What did families listen to in the past? Underline it.

⑤ Read Underline the sentence that tells what may happen in the future.

We use many of the same kinds of things that people used in the past.

Think about the future. Soon families may do things in a whole new way!

SHORT RESPONSE

Cite Text Evidence Reread pages 79–81. What is one way that family life has changed over time? Write it below.

_____

_ _

_____

_ _

_____

_ _

_____

Background Elephants are the largest animals living on land. Because elephants are so huge, other animals don't usually bother them.

Setting a Purpose Read the poem to find out something the author thinks might scare an elephant.

A Poem

by Langston Hughes

Read Together

①Read Underline what the elephant might be afraid of.

Elephant,

Elephant,

Big as a

House!

They tell me

That you

Are afraid of a

Mouse.

SHORT RESPONSE

Cite Text Evidence Reread the poem. What do you notice about the words <u>house</u> and <u>mouse</u>? Write it below.

_____

- -

_____

UNIT 5
Watch Us Grow

Background Bugs aren't always fun to have around, but some kinds of bugs are great to have in a garden. They help plants grow.

Setting a Purpose Read to find out what makes some bugs good garden helpers.

Garden Good Guys

Read Together

by **Timothy Thomas**

1 **Read** Underline the sentence that tells which bugs are garden good guys.

If you have a garden, you should know about bugs. Some bugs are **pests** that eat the plants. Other bugs eat the pests. They are the garden good guys!

If you want a healthy garden, make sure you have **ladybugs**. Ladybugs eat tiny bugs that snack on garden plants.

pests:

ladybug

2 **Reread** Reread page 87. What kind of bug is good for your garden? Write it below.

_____

- -

_____

③ **Read** Circle the picture of a praying mantis.

You may not think a praying mantis is as pretty as a ladybug, but it is a good garden friend. A **praying mantis** hunts and eats many garden pests.

The **big-eyed bug** is tiny. Can you guess how it got its name? Big-eyed bugs eat bugs that harm vegetables.

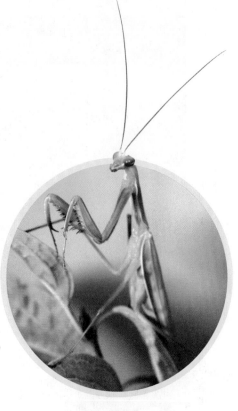

praying mantis

big-eyed bug

④ **Reread** Reread page 88. What does a big-eyed bug eat? Write it below.

_____

- -

_____

- -

_____

- -

_____

5 **R**ead Underline the sentence that tells what a dragonfly looks like.

The **dragonfly** has a long thin body, large eyes, and two sets of wings. Dragonflies are good for gardens and good for you, too. They eat garden pests <u>and</u> mosquitoes!

dragonfly

wing

SHORT RESPONSE

Cite Text Evidence Reread pages 87–89. What did you learn about one kind of helpful bug? Write it below.

_____

- - - - - - - - - - - - - - - - - - -

_____

- - - - - - - - - - - - - - - - - - -

_____

- - - - - - - - - - - - - - - - - - -

_____

Background Mother birds lay eggs. Then they sit on the eggs to keep them warm. That helps the eggs to hatch.

Setting a Purpose Read to find out about a special baby bird born in Mother Duck's nest.

The Ugly Duckling

Read Together

① **Read** Underline the words that tell when the story happens.

Once upon a time, a duck sat on eight eggs. One day, all but one of the eggs hatched. The ducks waited until the last baby bird came out. He was big and gray. The other ducks thought he was ugly.

② **Reread** Reread page 91. Find the detail that tells what the last baby bird looks like. Write it below.

_____

- -

_____

_____

- -

_____

③ **Read** How does the ugly duckling feel? Circle the word.

ducklings:

Each day the **ducklings** would follow Mother Duck. They were learning to be ducks. The other ducks did not want to play with the ugly duckling. He felt sad. One day he left.

Winter soon came. A farmer found the ugly duckling. "I must take you home before it begins to snow," he said.

④ **Reread** Where does the farmer take the ugly duckling? Write it below.

_____

- -

_____

_____

- -

_____

⑤ Read Underline the sentence that tells what happens to the swans at the end of the story.

When spring came, the farmer took the duckling to a pond. The duckling saw himself in the water. He felt like many years had passed. He had changed!

Now he knew he was not an ugly duckling. He was a young swan. He and the other swans lived happily ever after.

SHORT RESPONSE

Cite Text Evidence Reread pages 91–93. Why is the ugly duckling happy at the end of the story? Write it below.

_____

- -

_____

_____

- -

_____

Background Poems and songs are alike in many ways. This poem about a pet is also a folk song.

Setting a Purpose Read the poem to find out who has a pet and what the pet's name is.

Bingo

Read Together

1 **Read** Underline the two lines of the poem that have the same words.

There was a farmer had a dog,

And Bingo was his name, O!

B – I – N – G – O,

B – I – N – G – O,

B – I – N – G – O,

And Bingo was his name, O!

SHORT RESPONSE

Cite Text Evidence   Reread the poem. Who has a pet named Bingo? Write it below.

_____

- -

_____

- -

_____

- -

_____

Background Like many kinds of fruit, apples grow on trees. An apple tree begins as a seed. It takes a long time before it starts to grow apples!

Setting a Purpose Read to find out how a tiny apple seed grows and one day gives us tasty apples.

Grow, Apples, Grow!

Read Together

①Read Underline the detail that tells what the roots of an apple tree do.

Every apple tree starts with a tiny apple seed. An apple tree grows roots, which take in water and food from the soil. The apple tree also grows leaves, which make food from sunlight.

apple

seed

②Reread Reread page 97. What part of an apple tree makes food from sunlight? Write it below.

_____

- - - - - - - - - - - - - - - - - - - -

_____

_____

- - - - - - - - - - - - - - - - - - - -

_____

③ Read Underline the detail that tells what happens after apple blossoms fall off the tree.

In the spring, apple trees blossom, or grow flowers.

The flowers drop off, and apples grow in their place.

In the fall, the apples are ready to be picked.

People make many kinds of foods from apples.

④ Reread Reread page 98. Circle the season when apples are ready to be picked.

5 **Read** Underline the words that tell what apples can taste and feel like.

Apples may be sweet, or **tart**, or soft, or crisp, or crunchy. But one thing apples always are is

tart:

munchy,

munchy,

munchy!

SHORT RESPONSE

Cite Text Evidence Reread pages 97–99. What did you learn about apples? Write it below.

_____

- -

_____

- -

_____

- -

_____

- -

_____

Background Symbols are pictures, signs, or things that stand for something. You can learn about the United States by understanding some symbols of our country.

Setting a Purpose Read to find out about important places and things in our country.

Symbols of Our Country

by Agatha Jane

Read Together

① **Read** Underline the name of the capital of the United States.

We live in the United States of America. This city is Washington, D.C. It is the capital of the United States. You can see and learn a lot here. Let's go!

American Flag

The flag is a symbol of the United States. The red and white stripes stand for the first thirteen states. The stars stand for each state that is part of the United States now.

② **Reread** Reread page 101. What do the stripes on our flag stand for? Write it below.

_____

- -

_____

③ **Read** Circle the heading for this part of the text.

monument:

Washington Monument

George Washington was our first President. This tall building is named for him. This painting of George Washington is in the White House.

④ **Reread** Reread page 102. Who is the tall building in the picture named for? Write his name below.

_____

- - - - - - - - - - - - - - - - - - -

_____

⑤ Read Underline the word that tells what you can see at the Lincoln Memorial.

Lincoln Memorial

Abraham Lincoln was our sixteenth President. You can see his statue at the Lincoln Memorial.

White House

The President works and lives here. People from all states vote for the person they want to be President.

⑥ Reread Reread page 103. Who works and lives at the White House? Write the name below.

_____

- -

_____

7 **Read** Circle the heading that names the place where laws are made.

Capitol Building

Voters from each state elect people to represent them. This is where they make laws.

Supreme Court

Judges work here. They decide how laws should be followed.

8 **Reread** Reread page 104. Who works at the Supreme Court? Write it below.

_____

- -

_____

9 Read Underline the word that tells how people feel about our country.

You can see symbols of our country all over the United States. We are very proud of our country!

SHORT RESPONSE

Cite Text Evidence Reread pages 101–105. Tell something about one special symbol of our country. Write it below.

_____

- -

_____

- -

_____

- -

_____

UNIT 6
Three Cheers for Us!

Background There are many kinds of art! Some artists draw or paint pictures. Others make sculptures, or statues, out of wood, stone, or metal. Some artists even glue things together.

Setting a Purpose Read to find out about different artists and the art they make.

Read Together

Artists Create Art!

by Anne Rogers

1 Read Underline the word that tells one way that artists make pictures.

An artist makes art. Some artists paint pictures. Other artists make things.

2 **Read** Circle the name of the city where you can see the sculpture of the duck and her ducklings.

Nancy Schön made this mother duck and her **ducklings**. They are in a park in the city of Boston.

ducklings:

Nancy Schön's sculpture *Make Way for Ducklings* is in the Boston Public Garden.

3 **Reread** Reread page 109. What is the name of the sculpture in the photograph? Write it below.

_____

_____

④ Read Underline the sentence that tells where Georges Seurat studied art.

Georges Seurat went to art school in France. Look at his painting. Once you have studied it, you will see it is made of many brushstrokes. Are you surprised?

Seated Figures, Study for *A Sunday Afternoon on the Island of the Grande Jatte* by Georges Seurat

⑤ Reread Reread page 110. What is the painting made of? Write it below.

_____

_____

_____

Tressa "Grandma" Prisbrey used glass bottles to make her art. She learned by herself. No teacher helped her.

Grandma Prisbrey made a wishing well with bottles. She even made a building where her grandchildren played.

What kind of art would you like to make? Would you like to paint? Would you like to build something? There are many kinds of art!

SHORT RESPONSE

Cite Text Evidence Reread pages 108–111. Tell something you learned about one artist you read about. Write it below.

_____

- -

_____

Background The weather outside is always changing. The blowing wind makes the air feel cool. The bright sun makes it feel warm.

Setting a Purpose Read to find out what the characters learn in the story.

The Wind and the Sun

an Aesop's fable

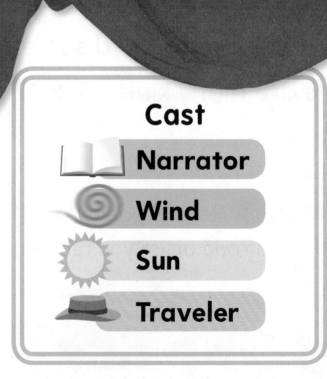

Cast
Narrator
Wind
Sun
Traveler

① **Read** Underline the detail that tells about the different ideas Wind and Sun have.

Narrator Sometimes stories teach a lesson. In this story, Wind and Sun have different ideas about who is stronger.

Wind I am stronger.

Sun No, I am stronger.

Wind That's enough **bragging**. Let's have a contest. I know **I** will win.

bragging:

Sun I'll be happy to have a contest.

② **Reread** Reread page 113. What will Wind and Sun do to decide who is right? Write it below.

_____

_____

③ **Read** Look for the sentence that tells how to win the contest. Underline it.

Wind Okay. I see a traveler coming near. Whoever gets the traveler to take off that coat is stronger.

Narrator First Wind began to blow very hard. Once Wind started, it did not stop.

Traveler That wind is always so cold. I need to wrap my coat tight around me.

④ **Reread** Reread page 114. What does Wind do to try to win the contest? Write it below.

_____

_____

_____

_____

⑤ Read Underline the detail that tells the lesson this story teaches.

📖 **Narrator** Then Sun began to shine from high up in the sky. It was shining gently. The air got warmer and warmer.

🎩 **Traveler** Now it's nice and warm. I can take off my heavy coat.

📖 **Narrator** The moral is: "It is better to use kindness instead of force."

SHORT RESPONSE

Cite Text Evidence Reread pages 113–115. Who is stronger, Wind or Sun? Tell why. Write it below.

_____

- -

_____

- -

_____

Background We use different tools to get information about the weather. The tools can give us facts about the wind, the rain, and the temperature.

Setting a Purpose Read to find out about tools people use to measure weather.

Measuring Weather

Read Together

①Read Underline the sentence that tells what a windsock does.

There are different tools for measuring weather.

Have you ever heard of a windsock? It shows which way the wind blows.

A rain **gauge** measures how much rain falls. A large storm will bring a lot of rain.

gauge:

②Reread Reread page 117. Find what a rain gauge measures. Write it below.

_____

- -

_____

_____

- -

_____

③ **Read** Look for the sentence that tells what <u>temperature</u> means. Underline it.

A thermometer measures temperature. Temperature is how warm or cool something is.

On a hot day, you and your friends might like to ride bikes or play ball.

④ **Reread** Reread page 118. Find two things you might do on a hot day. Write them below.

_____

- - - - - - - - - - - - - - - - - -

_____

_____

- - - - - - - - - - - - - - - - - -

_____

⑤ Read Underline the word that names what you might wear on a cold day.

On a cold day, you might want to put on a coat and play in the leaves or build a snowman.

When you know the temperature, you know what to wear.

⑥ Reread Reread page 119. How can knowing the temperature help you? Write it below.

_____

_____

_____

_____

⑦ Read Underline the detail that explains what each bar on the graph shows.

Look at the bars across the graph. Each bar shows the temperature for a day.

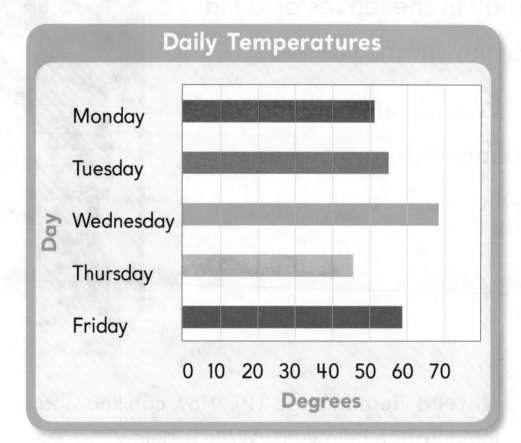

Daily Temperatures

Monday

Tuesday

Wednesday

Thursday

Friday

Day

0 10 20 30 40 50 60 70

Degrees

⑧ Reread Reread page 120. On what day was the temperature almost 60 degrees? Write it below.

_____

- -

_____

9. Read Find two words that have opposite meanings. Circle them.

Which day was the hottest?
Which day was the coolest?
What was the temperature on
the second day of the week?

SHORT RESPONSE

Cite Text Evidence   Reread pages 117–121. What did you learn about measuring the weather? Write it below.

_____

- - - - - - - - - - - - - - - - - - -

_____

_____

- - - - - - - - - - - - - - - - - - -

_____

Background Different kinds of bugs do different things. Some bugs fly fast, some crawl along slowly, and some make sounds.

Setting a Purpose Read the poem to find out different things that bugs do.

Read Together

Song of the Bugs

by Margaret Wise Brown

① **Read** Circle the word that rhymes with <u>creep</u>.

Some bugs pinch

And some bugs creep

Some bugs buzz themselves to sleep

Buzz Buzz Buzz Buzz

This is the song of the bugs.

Some bugs fly

When the moon is high

Some bugs make a light in the sky

Flicker, flicker firefly

This is the song of the bugs.

SHORT RESPONSE

Cite Text Evidence Reread the poem. What is one thing that some bugs do? Write it below.

_____

- -

_____

- -

_____

Background A team is a group of people who do something together. For a team to do well, everyone on the team should be a good team player.

Setting a Purpose Read to find out what a good team player does.

Be a Team Player

①Read Look for four kinds of games that teams play. Circle them.

Have you ever loved playing on a team? Most people have lots of fun on a team.

All kinds of people play on teams. Sisters and brothers play. Friends and cousins play.

There are all kinds of teams. Some people play baseball or basketball. Some play soccer or volleyball. People may play on a field or on a **court**.

court:

②Reread Reread page 125. Find two places where teams play. Underline them.

125

③ Read Underline the detail that tells what you should <u>not</u> do if you lose a game.

No matter what kind of team it is, it's important to be a good team player. Try not to feel sorry if you lose a game. Everyone loses sometimes. It's only important to try your best and have fun.

④ Reread Reread page 126. What is more important than whether you win or lose a game?

_____

- - - - - - - - - - - - - - - - -

_____

_____

- - - - - - - - - - - - - - - - -

_____

5 **Read** Circle the name of the person who team players listen to.

Here is a checklist of things to remember when you play on a team.

Be a Team Player.

✓ Pay attention to the coach.
✓ Follow the rules.
✓ Do your best.
✓ Don't quit.
✓ Have fun!

SHORT RESPONSE

Cite Text Evidence   Reread pages 125–127. What is something a good team player should do? Write it below.

_____

- -

_____

- -

_____

Acknowledgments

"Elephant, Elephant" from *The Sweet and Sour Animal Book* by Langston Hughes. Text copyright © 1994 by The Estate of Langston Hughes. Reprinted by permission of Oxford University Press, Inc. and Harold Ober Associates Incorporated.

"Jambo" from *Nightfeathers* by Sundaira Morninghouse. Text copyright © 1989 by Sundaira Morninghouse. Reprinted by permission of Open Hand Publishing LLC. *www.openhand.com*

"Song of the Bugs" from *Nibble, Nibble* by Margaret Wise Brown. Text copyright © 1959 by William R. Scott, Inc. Text copyright renewed © 1987 by Roberta Brown Rauch. Reprinted by permission of HarperCollins Publishers.